FLUTE / CD

www.fabermusic.com/groovelab

© 2002 by Faber Music Ltd
First published in 2002 by Faber Music Ltd
3 Queen Square London WC1N 3AU
Cover by velladesign
Music processed by Don Sheppard
Printed in England by Caligraving Ltd

CD recorded in the lavalounge, September 2001–May 2002
Andy Hampton: sax, clarinet, flute, keyboards
David Motion: samplers, synthesizers
Phillip Littlemore: trumpet, flugel horn
Kathryn Oswald: flute
Ilan Rog: drum loops
Produced by David Motion and Andy Hampton
Programmed by David Motion
℗ 2002 Faber Music Ltd
© 2002 Faber Music Ltd

ISBN 0-571-52120-7

To buy Faber Music publications or to find out about the full range of titles available
please contact your local music retailer or Faber Music sales enquiries:

Faber Music Limited, Burnt Mill, Elizabeth Way, Harlow, CM20 2HX England
Tel: +44 (0)1279 82 89 82   Fax: +44 (0)1279 82 89 83
sales@fabermusic.com   www.fabermusic.com

Groovelab

4

Amsterdam David Motion

Amsterdam (with improvisation) David Motion

Wot's the buzz? Andy Hampton

Wot's the buzz? (with improvisation) Andy Hampton

8

5 # Deep cover David Motion

Deep cover (with improvisation) David Motion

Didgeri blues Andy Hampton

Didgeri blues (with improvisation) Andy Hampton

Brick Lane David Motion

Brick Lane (with improvisation) David Motion

Marimba Heaven Andy Hampton

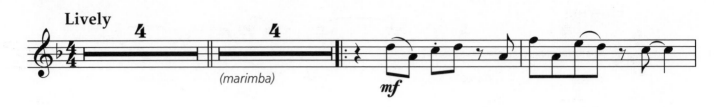

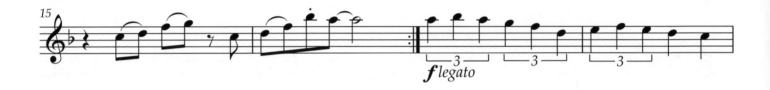

Marimba Heaven (with improvisation) Andy Hampton

Overload David Motion

Overload (with improvisation) David Motion

Left for Swindon
Andy Hampton

Left for Swindon (with improvisation) Andy Hampton

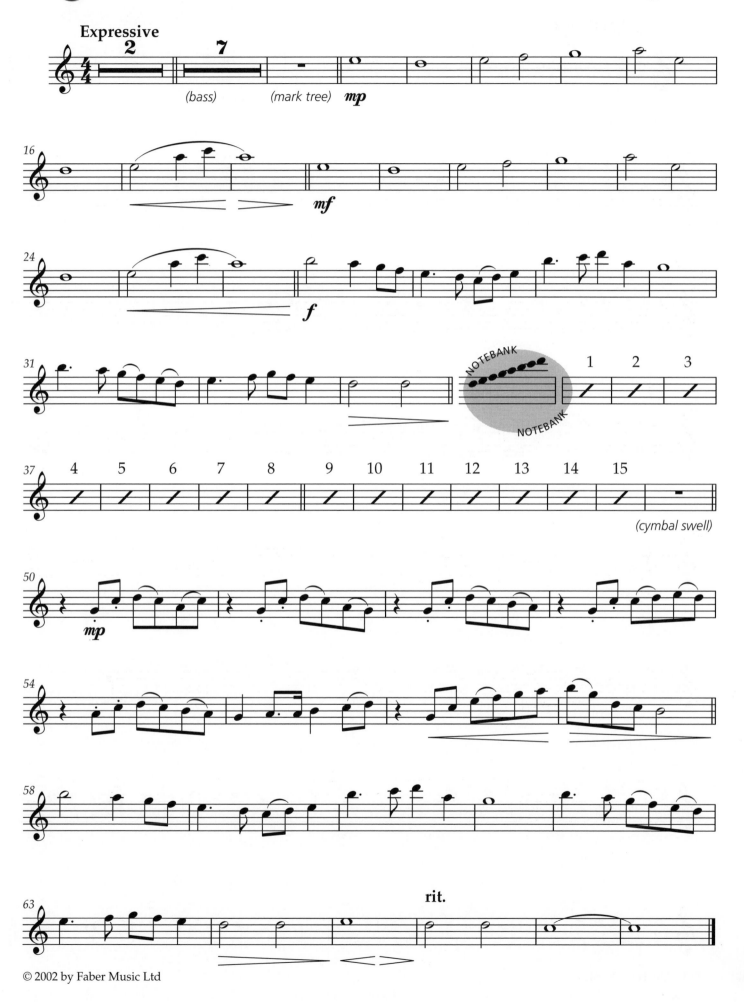

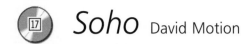

Soho David Motion

Laid-back

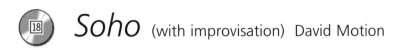

Soho (with improvisation) David Motion

Yer dinner's in the dog Andy Hampton

Yer dinner's in the dog (with improvisation) Andy Hampton

GROOVE LAB